THE PRACTICAL GUIDE TO MICRO AND MACRO ECONOMICS

300 + Easy to Understand Definitions with Examples and Graphs

Table of Contents

Introduction

Economics 101

More Macroeconomics Concepts

Macro Policy and Finance

Economic Growth

Aggregate Supply and Demand

Tax and Fiscal Policy

Most Common Graphs and their Definitions

INTRODUCTION

I have been inspired to write The Practical Guide to Micro and Macro Economics by my students. I have yet to come across a student that did not seem perplexed by the plethora of definitions concocted by ivory-tower elites to say the obvious. I always tell my students to think of their everyday life. Do you have a hobby? Do you like to shop? Do you like sports? Do you enjoy traveling and meeting new people? Then you are interested in Economics. Once I gauge my students, I give examples that pertain to their lives and show them how this seemingly convoluted term is actually a basic tenet of our everyday existence.

A good example is taking one of the most complicated terms in economics: **Nash Equilibrium.** I ask my students to think of the current cell phone providers. These days nearly every person has a cellular phone and definitely my high school and universities students. In fact, they would rather pay their phone bills before they would pay for insurance, gas or food. The phone has become an integral part of our lives. Then I ask them to name all the cell phone providers. Once we write down the four providers we then try to evaluate and see what differences exist between them? How do they try to compete with one another? The end result of course is a great analogy for Nash's Equilibrium.

This book is meant to simplify and inspire readers to find an interest in economics. The book also serves as a reference guide for students of economics. It is a useful guide when studying for an AP exam or Economics tests.

To distinguish between Macro and Micro Economics just think of it in these terms:

Micro means small or particular

Macro means large or whole

Example:

Microeconomics would be dealing with your choices of where to buy the newest Apple I-Phone. Should you buy it at the local Verizon or AT&T store or go to the Apple Store or order online.

Macroeconomics would be dealing with the global distribution of the Apple I-Phone and its relationships to the international technology markets as a whole.

Here is a more detailed explanation:

- **Microeconomics** is the study of particular markets, and segments of the economy. It looks at issues such as consumer behavior, individual labor markets, and the theory of firms.
- **Macroeconomics** is the study of the whole economy. It looks at 'aggregate' variables, such as aggregate demand, national output and inflation.

Micro economics is concerned with:

- Supply and demand in individual markets
- Individual consumer behavior. E.g. Consumer choice theory
- Individual labor markets – e.g. demand for labor, wage determination
- Externalities arising from production and consumption.

Macroeconomics is concerned with

- Monetary / fiscal policy. E.g. what effect does interest rates have on whole economy?
- Reasons for inflation, and unemployment
- Economic Growth
- International trade and globalization
- Reasons for differences in living standards and economic growth between countries.
- Government borrowing

ECONOMICS 101

1. **Economics** is the study of how people or societies satisfy wants with limited or scarce resources.
2. **Scarcity** is the condition where unlimited human wants face limited resources.
3. There is no such thing as a free lunch (**TINSTAAFL**).
4. **Three basic questions:** What must we produce? How should we produce it? For whom should we produce?
5. **Macroeconomics** is the study of the economy as a whole (forest)
6. **Microeconomics** is the study of individual parts of the economy (trees).
7. **Factors of Production: Land** (Natural Resources), **Labor** (Human Capital), **Capital** (Tools, Machinery, Plant), and **Entrepreneurs** (Risk-Taker who combines land, labor, and capital) produce goods and services. Also known as economic resources, economic inputs, or scarce resources.
8. **Goods** are items that satisfy an economic want.
9. **Consumer goods** (iPods, LCD TVs, Barbie Dolls) are final goods purchased by households (consumers).
10. **Capital goods** (Machinery, Robots, and Hammer) are goods purchased by businesses to produce consumer goods.
11. **Durable goods** last more than 3 years (Car, Washer, and Dryer) and can be repaired. These goods suffer most during recessions.
12. **Nondurable goods** generally last less than 3 years (Lettuce, Pens, Loose-leaf paper, Coffee).
13. **Services** (Haircut, Legal advice, Surgery, Painting) are work performed for someone and are intangible.
14. **Value** is worth expressed in dollars and cents. To have value it must also have **Utility,** a good's or services capacity to provide satisfaction. **Wealth** is the accumulation of goods that are tangible, scarce, useful, and transferable to another person.

15. **Circular Flow Model:** The flow of inputs and money through the factor market and flow of goods/services through the product market.
16. **Productivity** is a measure of the amount of output produced by the amount of inputs within a certain time. Investing in capital improves productivity and leads to economic growth.
17. **Price Level:** The overall level of prices in a country, as usually measured empirically by a price index, but often captured in theoretical models by a single variable. Just remember that this is a measurement of prices for goods and services.
18. **Trade-offs** are the alternative choices people face in making an economic decision.
19. **Opportunity Cost** is the cost of the next best alternative among a person's choices (Do I chat on Facebook all night or do my economics homework?)
20. **Production Possibilities Curve:** A PPC or Production Possibilities Frontier is a simplified economic model that illustrates the concept of opportunity cost. We assume an economy can use their resources to produce only two goods. Resources and technology are fixed, and the economy can never produce outside of the PPC (Point X) in the present. If the economy is currently producing at a point on the PPC (Point E) then it is experiencing full employment. However, if the economy is producing at a point inside the PPC (Point U), then there are resources that are currently unemployed.

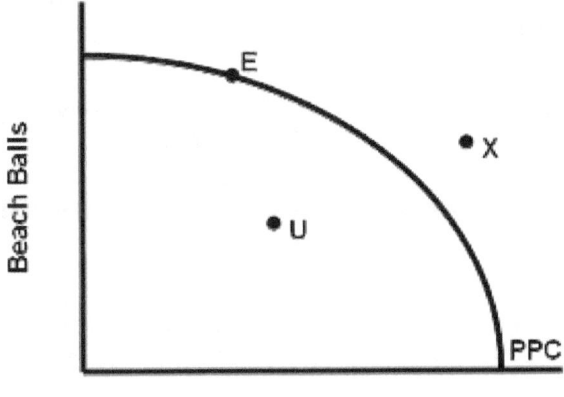

21.

22. When the PPC shifts out (to the right), economic growth has occurred. The factors that lead to growth are increased quantity and quality of resources, increased productivity, improved technology, and better education and training.

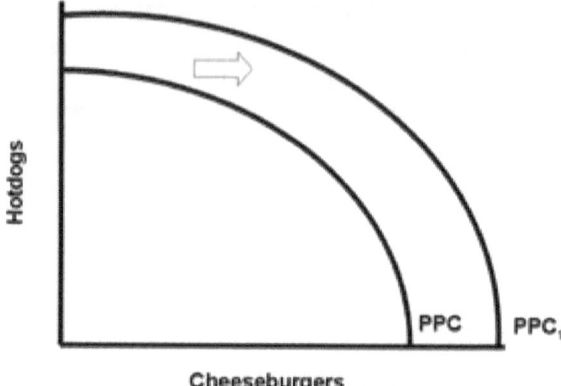

23.
24. **Law of Increasing Costs:** Explains why the PPC is bowed outward (Concave) from the origin. To produce more of one good, an economy must sacrifice ever-increasing quantities of the other good.
25. **Constant Opportunity Cost PPC** occurs when the PPC is a straight line. The opportunity cost of producing an additional good remains the same.
26. **Absolute Advantage** is when one country can produce more of a good than the other country.
27. **Comparative Advantage:** considers the opportunity cost and shows how everyone gains through trade. If a country can produce a good at a lower opportunity cost then it has the comparative advantage.
28. **Economic Goals:** Freedom, efficiency, equity, security, employment, price stability, and growth.
29. **Traditional Economies:** Roles and economic decisions are defined by custom. Everyone knows which role to play. Discourages new ideas which leads to lower standard of living (poor health, poor education).
30. **Command Economies:** Central authority determines the WHAT, HOW, and FOR WHOM to produce. Allows for quick change with basic services at low cost but consumer needs may not be met.

31. **Market Economies:** Producers and consumers determine the three questions. In a market transaction consumers cast their "dollar votes." Market economies can adjust to change, have a high degree of individual freedom and small degree of government involvement, and have a high variety of goods and services, and high degree of consumer satisfaction. It cannot meet every person's basic needs and the people face a high level of personal uncertainty. There is also the prospect of economic failure. A few examples include US, Canada, and Japan.
32. **Consumer Sovereignty:** Consumers rule! Remember "dollar votes?"
33. **Law of Demand:** An inverse relationship between price and quantity demanded. When the price of a good changes then quantity demanded changes (point-to-point movement along the curve).
34. **Determinants of Demand:** These are the non-price determinants or shift factors of the entire demand curve; Consumer tastes and preferences, Number of buyers or market size, Income, Prices of substitute goods, Prices of complementary goods, and Future price expectations.
35. **Inferior Good:** As income increases demand for an inferior good (Chef Boyardee, Ramen noodles) decreases (shifts left).
36. **Normal Good:** As income increases demand for a normal good (Steak) increases (shifts right).
37. **Law of Supply:** A direct relationship exists between price and quantity supplied. As P increases QS increases; a change in price will lead to a change in quantity supplied (point-to-point movement along a supply curve).
38. **Determinants of Supply:** These are the shift factors for the supply curve; Resource prices (lower costs increase supply), Technology, Productivity, Taxes (reduce the incentive to produce) & subsidies (are incentives to produce more), Price expectations (if prices expected to fall in future, supply increases in the present), and Prices of goods that use the same production techniques (Cucumbers and Watermelon).
39. **Market Equilibrium** or market clearing price is the point where the demand and supply curves meet. A **surplus** occurs when the price is greater than equilibrium (QS > QD) and a

shortage occurs when the price is less than equilibrium (QD > QS).
40. **Price floors** and **price ceilings** are price controls (limits) that can be set by the government.
41. **Effective price ceiling** is a maximum legal price that must be set below the equilibrium price (leads to a shortage of the good).
42. **Effective price floor** is a minimum legal price that must be set above the equilibrium price (leads to a surplus of the good).
43. **Sole Proprietorship:** Business run by one person. They are the smallest, but most numerous and profitable types of businesses. Advantages: Easy start-up, easy management, owner gets all profits, business itself pays no income taxes (only business owner's personal income is taxed), psychological satisfaction of owning a business, and easy to close. Disadvantages: Owner has unlimited liability, hard to raise financial capital, might be difficult to hire personnel or stock enough inventory, owner might have limited managerial experience, hard to attract qualified employees, limited life, and business dies when owner dies or sells the business.
44. **Partnerships:** Business jointly owned by two or more persons. They are the least numerous and has the second smallest proportion of sales and net income. Advantages: easy start-up, easy management, **no special taxes on partnership**, easier to raise financial capital, larger size, and easier to attract skilled employees. Disadvantages: Partners responsible for acts of all the partners, limited life if a partner leaves, and potential for partner conflicts.
45. **General Partnership:** All partners are involved in the management and sales.
46. **Limited Partnership:** At least one partner is not involved in management - That partner may have helped to finance the business.
47. **Corporations:** A business organization recognized by law as a separate legal entity with all the rights of an individual. They receive a **charter** (permission from government) to create a corporation that includes details of **stock**

ownership. Investors who buy common/preferred stock are the owners of the firm. Advantages: Ease of raising capital, professionals may run the firm, owners have limited liability, business life is unlimited, and easy to transfer ownership. Disadvantages: A charter is expensive, ownership and management are separated so shareholders have little say in running the business, corporate income is taxed twice, and subject to government regulation.

48. **Gross Domestic Product** is the market value of all final goods and services produced in a nation in one year. It is considered to be the most important measurement of production and output. GDP counts only **final goods and services** - not intermediate goods and services.
49. GDP does not include second hand sales, buying and selling of stocks/bonds (financial transactions), transfer payments (public and private), unemployment compensation, and certain interest payments.
50. GDP includes profits earned by foreign owned businesses and income earned by foreigners in the United States, but excludes profits earned by US-owned companies overseas and income earned by US citizens abroad (this would be in the **GNP** which was used as the basic measurement of output until 1991).
51. GDP can be calculated through adding up all expenditures (**GDP = C + Ig + G + Xn**) or by adding up all incomes received by owners of productive resources.
52. Consumption (C) is the largest component of GDP through the expenditures approach
53. Wages and Salaries represent the largest component of GDP through the income approach
54. Other measures include: **Net Domestic Product, National Income, Personal Income, and Disposable Income.**
55. **Net Domestic Product** is GDP minus depreciation
56. **National income** is earned by all US resource suppliers.
57. **Personal income** is income that can be spent, saved, or taxed.
58. **Disposable income** can be spent or saved.
59. **Business Cycle** shows the ups and downs of economic activity over a period of years. The phases

are **expansion/recovery, peak, contraction/recession,** and **trough**.
60. **Price indexes** are used to measure price changes in our economy. We compare the prices of a given "**market basket**" of goods and services in one year with the prices of the same "market basket" in another year. A price index has a base year of 100 - the price level in all other years is expressed as a percentage of the price level in the base year.
61. **Price index = (Current year prices/Base year prices) x 100**
62. The most frequently used price indexes are the **Consumer Price Index (CPI), Producer Price Index (PPI),** and the **GDP Deflator**.
63. Percentage changes can be calculated (New index - Old index)/(Old index) X 100
64. **Real GDP** is adjusted for price changes and **Nominal GDP** is not adjusted for price changes.
65. **Inflation** is the general increase in the overall price level. Savers, lenders, and people on fixed incomes are hurt by inflation. Borrowers or people that make fixed payments gain from unanticipated inflation.
66. **Fisher Equation:** Real percentage change = Nominal percentage change - Inflation rate
67. **Rule of 70**: uses a percentage to predict how long it takes for a number to double (70/10% inflation = 7 years)
68. **Unemployment Rate** is the percentage of the labor force that cannot find work (# unemployed/#labor force) x 100
69. There are four types of unemployment: **frictional, structural, seasonal,** and **cyclical**.
70. **Frictional unemployment** occurs when someone quits a job to seek employment elsewhere, is fired, or if a college grad begins looking for work. It is short-term or temporary.
71. **Structural unemployment** occurs when someone's job skills are no longer in demand; like a robotic arm that replaces an automobile worker. When this happens, the worker has to retrain or move to find employment.
72. **Cyclical unemployment** occurs when someone loses a job due to a contraction of the business cycle or recession.
73. Frictional and structural employment always exist - even when the economy is operating at **full employment**

74. The **Aggregate Demand (AD)** and **Aggregate Supply (AS)** curves are used to illustrate changes in real output and the price level of an economy.
75. Aggregate Demand curve is downward and can be explained by the wealth effect, the income effect, and the foreign purchases effect.
76. **Determinants of AD** are changes in consumer spending, investment spending, government spending, and net export spending. Changes in these areas will shift the AD curve and change the price level and real output/GDP.
77. Aggregate Supply curve can be divided into 3 ranges: horizontal or **Keynesian range**, upward sloping or **intermediate range**, and the vertical or **classical range**.
78. **Determinants of AS** are changes in input prices, productivity, legal environment, and quantity of available resources. These will shift the AS curve and change real GDP and the price level.
79. Changes in output can also be shown on the Keynesian Cross Model or Expenditures Model, however the price level remains constant.
80. **Autonomous spending** is the part of AD that is independent of the current rate of economic activity & induced spending depends on the current rate of economic activity.
81. The **multiplier** is a number that influences the relationship of changes in autonomous spending to changes in real GDP. **Multiplier = 1/MPS or 1/1-MPC**.
82. **Keynesian economists** believe that equilibrium levels of GDP can occur at less than or more than full-employment level of GDP. Classical economists believe that long-run equilibrium can occur only at full employment.
83. **Fiscal Policy** consists of government actions that may increase or decrease AD. The two actions are changes in government spending and taxes.
84. **Expansionary Fiscal Policy's** purpose is to increase AD. The government could increase government spending and/or decrease taxes.
85. **Contractionary Fiscal Policy** is used to decrease AD during a period of inflation. The government could increase taxes and/or decrease its spending.

86. **Discretionary Fiscal Policy** is when the government must take action or pass laws to change spending and taxation.
87. **Automatic stabilizers** change government spending or taxes without new laws or actions taken.
88. The **balanced budget multiplier** shows that equal increases or decreases in taxes and government spending increase or decrease equilibrium GDP by an amount equal to that increase or decrease.
89. **Stagflation** can be explained by a decrease in AS.
90. **Money** should have portability, acceptability, durability, divisibility, and stability in value.
91. **The four basic types of money** throughout history are: commodity money, representative money, fiat money, and checkbook money.
92. **Money** has three functions: **medium of exchange, standard of value,** and **store of value**
93. **M1** consists of checkable deposits, traveler's checks, and currency. Checkable deposits make up about 75% of M1 and are also called demand deposits.
94. **M2** and **M3** are broader definitions of money and include savings accounts and other time deposits.
95. **Velocity** is the number of times per year the money supply is used to make payments for final goods and services.
96. The equation of exchange is **MV=PQ** or money x velocity = price x quantity. PQ is the nominal GDP.
97. **Banks** create money when they make loans. One bank's loan becomes another bank's demand deposit. Money is destroyed when the loan is repaid.
98. Banks must keep a percentage of their deposits as reserves. **Reserves** can be currency in the bank vault or deposits at the Federal Reserve Banks. The reserve requirement limits the amount of money the bank can create.
99. **Money Multiplier = 1/Reserve requirement**
100. The higher the **reserve requirement** the less money that can be created and vice versa.
101. **The Federal Reserve** has 3 tools to control the money supply: **open market operations** (buying and selling government bonds), changing the **discount rate**, and changing the **reserve requirement.**

102. **Expansionary/"Easy" monetary policy** could consist of decreasing the reserve requirement, decreasing the discount rate, and/or buying bonds on the open market. Often this is used to battle unemployment.
103. **Contractionary/"Tight" monetary policy** could consist of increasing the reserve requirement, increasing the discount rate, and/or selling bonds on the open market. The Fed follows a tight monetary policy during times of inflation.
104. Open market transactions are the most frequently used tool. The reserve requirement is the most powerful and rarely used.
105. **Monetarists** believe that money directly affects the economy through the equation of exchange and the money supply should increase by the same amount as the GDP (3-5% per year).
106. **Keynesians** believe that money affects interest rates which in turn affect investment and GDP. Easy money decreases interest rates and increases GDP during recessions. Tight money increases interest rates, which decreases AD and helps fight inflation.
107. **The Fed** cannot target both the money supply and interest rate simultaneously so it must choose which goal to strive for wisely.
108. Money should have portability, acceptability, durability, divisibility, and stability in value.
109. **The four basic types of money** throughout history are: commodity money, representative money, fiat money, and checkbook money.
110. Money has three functions: **medium of exchange, standard of value,** and **store of value**
111. **M1** consists of checkable deposits, traveler's checks, and currency. Checkable deposits make up about 75% of M1 and are also called demand deposits.
112. **M2** and **M3** are broader definitions of money and include savings accounts and other time deposits.
113. Velocity is the number of times per year the money supply is used to make payments for final goods and services.
114. The equation of exchange is **MV=PQ** or money x velocity = price x quantity. PQ is the nominal GDP.

115. Banks create money when they make loans. One bank's loan becomes another bank's demand deposit. Money is destroyed when the loan is repaid.
116. Banks must keep a percentage of their deposits as reserves. **Reserves** can be currency in the bank vault or deposits at the Federal Reserve Banks. The reserve requirement limits the amount of money the bank can create.
117. **Money Multiplier = 1/Reserve requirement**
118. The higher the reserve requirement the less money that can be created and vice versa.
119. **Federal Reserve** has 3 tools to control the money supply: **open market operations** (buying and selling government bonds), changing the **discount rate**, and changing the **reserve requirement.**
120. **Expansionary/"Easy" monetary policy** could consist of decreasing the reserve requirement, decreasing the discount rate, and/or buying bonds on the open market. Often this is used to battle unemployment.
121. **Contractionary/"Tight" monetary policy** could consist of increasing the reserve requirement, increasing the discount rate, and/or selling bonds on the open market. The Fed follows a tight monetary policy during times of inflation.
122. Open market transactions are the most frequently used tool. The reserve requirement is the most powerful and rarely used.
123. **Monetarists** believe that money directly affects the economy through the equation of exchange and the money supply should increase by the same amount as the GDP (3-5% per year).
124. **Keynesians** believe that money affects interest rates which in turn affect investment and GDP. Easy money decreases interest rates and increases GDP during recessions. Tight money increases interest rates, which decreases AD and helps fight inflation.
125. The Fed cannot target both the money supply and interest rate simultaneously so it must choose which goal to strive for wisely.
126. **Crowding out** is the effect of a rise in interest rates caused by increased borrowing by the federal government. Higher interest rates "crowd out" consumer and business borrowing.

Interactions between monetary policy and fiscal policy can affect overall AD - an expansionary fiscal policy with a tight monetary policy can cause "crowding out."

127. The **Phillips Curve** illustrates the inflation unemployment tradeoff and how this tradeoff differs in the short-run and long-run. The inverse relationship between unemployment rate and inflation when graphically charted is called the Phillips curve. William Phillips pioneered the concept first in his paper "The Relation between Unemployment and the Rate of Change of Money Wage Rates in the United Kingdom, 1861-1957,' in 1958. This theory is now proven for all major economies of the world.

128. **Economic growth** is measured by changed in real GDP and/or by changes in real GDP per capita.

129. **Economic growth** is concerned with increasing an economy's total productive capacity at full employment. This output is represented by a vertical long-run AS curve so economic growth can be shown as a rightward shift of a nation's LRAS curve or rightward shift of its PPC.

130.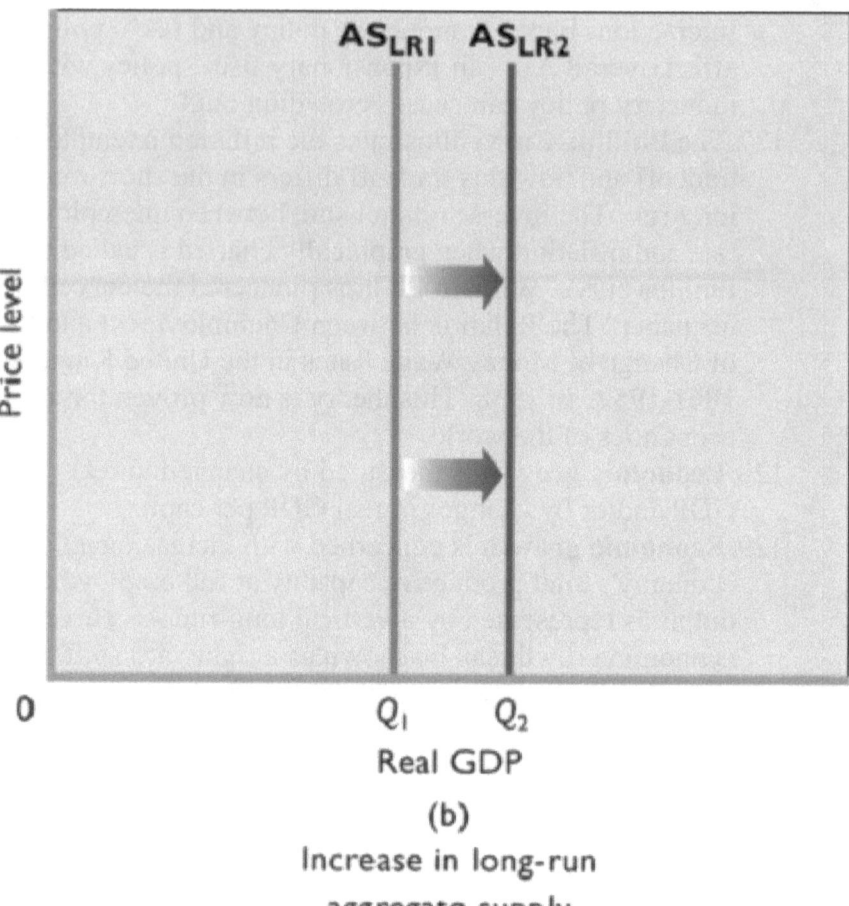

(b)
Increase in long-run aggregate supply

131. The **Keynesian model** is based on the belief that fiscal policy works through AD. Monetary policy works through interest rates and investment which also affects AD.
132. The **Classical model** represents an idealized version of a private-enterprise economy where AD/AS together determine the price level.
133. The **Monetarist model** focuses on changes in the money supply - remember MV=PQ.
134. **Supply-Side** economics emphasizes factors that because the AS curve to shift. Inflation and stagflation are caused by decreases in AS not AD. They recommend microeconomic

solutions like less government intervention and improved productivity.
135. People and nations trade to improve their standard of living (HDG #5) therefore both parties must gain from the trade.
136. Voluntary trade promotes economic progress because people **specialize** in what they do best.
137. **Comparative advantage** explains why there are mutual gains from specialization and trade. The nation with the lower opportunity cost for producing a product has the comparative advantage.
138. A nation has the **absolute advantage** if it can produce more of a good using the same amount of resources.
139. **Tariffs** and **quotas** are trade barriers that limit the potential gains from trade. They generally protect domestic sellers at the expense of domestic buyers and reduce efficiency in the allocation of scarce resources.
140. The **balance of payments** is a broader measure of international transactions. Considers all international account, capital account, and official reserves.
141. To trade nations must exchange currencies - **exchange rate** is the price of one currency in terms of another, and set up by supply and demand.
142. **Appreciation** is an increase in the value of a nation's currency in foreign exchange markets - tends to reduce exports and increase imports.
143. **Depreciation** is a decrease in the value of a nation's currency - tends to increase exports and decrease imports.
144. Monetary and fiscal policies can affect exchange rates and international balance of payments.

MORE MACROECONOMICS DEFINITIONS

145. **Bartering**: The trading of one good for another. This requires the double Coincidence of wants, a condition met when two individuals each have different goods that the other wants.

146. **Commodity Money**: Money that has an intrinsic value, that is, value beyond any value given to it because it is money. An example of this would be a gold coin that has value because it is a precious metal.

147. **Compound Interest**: Interest that is paid on a sum of money where the interest paid is added to the principal for the future calculation of interest. Click here to see the Formula.

148. **Consumption**: The purchase and use of goods and services by consumers.

149. **Currency**: The form of money used in a country.

150. **Defaulting on the Loan**: When a borrower fails to repay a loan leaving the lender without the money loaned.

151. **Demand for Money**: The amount of currency that consumers use for the purchase of goods and services. This varies depending mainly upon the price level.

152. **Equilibrium**: The state in a market when supply equals demand.

153. **Fiat Money**: Money that has no intrinsic value, that is, its only value comes from the fact that a governing body backs and regulates the currency.

154. **Fischer Effect**: The point for point relationship between changes in the money supply and changes in the inflation rate.

155. **Inflation**: The increase of the price level over time.

156. **Interest:** Money paid by a borrower to a lender for the use of a sum of money.

157. **Interest Rates**: The percent of the amount borrowed paid each year to the lender by the borrower in return for the use of the money.

158. **Liquidity**: The ease with which something of value can be exchanged for the currency of an economy.

159. **Medium of Exchange**: An item used commonly to trade for goods and services.

160. **Money Supply**: The quantity of money in an economy. In the US this is controlled through policy by the Fed.

161. **Nominal GDP**: The total value of all goods and services produced in a country valued at current prices.

162. **Nominal Interest**: The percent of the amount borrowed paid each year to the lender by the borrower in return for the use of the money not taking inflation into account.

163. **Nominal Value**: The value of something in current dollars without taking into account the effects of inflation.

164. **Output**: The amount of goods and services produced within an economy.

165. **Price Level**: The overall level of prices of goods and services in an economy. This is used in the calculation of inflation rates.

166. **Purchasing Power**: The real value of a dollar. This describes the quantity of goods and services that can be purchased for a dollar, taking into account the effects of inflation.

167. **Quantity Theory of Money**: The theory that says that the value of money is based on the amount of money in circulation, that is, the money supply.

168. **Real Interest**: The percent of the amount borrowed paid each year to the lender by the borrower in return for the use of the money adjusted for inflation.

169. **Real Value**: The value of something in taking into account the effects of inflation.

170. **Store of Value**: A good that holds a value in such a way that its price is fairly insensitive inflation.

171. **Unit of Account**: Something that is used universally in the description of money matters such as prices. The unit of account most commonly used in the US is the dollar.

172. **Value of Money**: The purchasing power of the dollar. The amount of goods and services that can be purchased for a fixed amount of money.

173. **Velocity**: The speed with which a dollar bill changes hands. The higher the velocity of money, the quicker that a given piece of currency will be traded for goods and services.

174. **Wage**: The amount of money paid to workers by employers valued in current dollars.

175. **Velocity of Money**: $M * V = P * Y$ where M is the money supply, V is the velocity, P is the price level, and Y is the quantity of output. $P * Y$, the price level multiplied by the quantity of output, gives the nominal GDP. This equation can be rearranged as $V = $ (nominal GDP) $/ M$. It can also be converted into a percentage change formula as (percent change in the money supply) + (percent change in velocity) = (percent change in the price level) + (percent change in output).

176. **Compound Interest:** First, calculate the value of the loan, by adding one to the interest rate, raising it to the number of years for the loan, and multiplying it by the loan amount. Then, to calculate the amount of interest, simply subtract the original loan amount from the total due.

177. **Real Interest Rate:** The real interest rate is equal to the nominal interest rate minus the inflation rate.

MACRO POLICY AND FINANCE

178. **100% Reserve Banking System**: A system in which banks must keep all deposits on hand and ready for withdrawal.
179. **Assets**: Cash, stocks, bonds, and physical goods that are stores of wealth and value.
180. **Balance Sheet**: An accounting tool where assets and liabilities are compared side by side.
181. **Borrowers**: Individuals who take out loans from banks.
182. **Currency:** Money, either fiat or commodity that is commonly used in an economy.
183. **Demand Deposits**: Deposits made by in banks that can be withdrawn at any time--that is, on demand.
184. **Deposits**: Money given to banks for safekeeping and to earn interest.
185. **Federal Deposit Insurance Corporation**: A corporation that insures individual bank accounts up to $100,000 to ensure that the public is confident in the banking system.
186. **Federal Funds Interest Rate**: The discount interest rate at which the branch banks of the Fed loan money to other banks.
187. **Federal Reserve**: The federal group that controls the money supply though monetary policy and fiscal policy.
188. **Federal Reserve Banks**: Branches of the Fed that serve as banks for non-government controlled banks by accepting deposits, giving withdrawals, and making loans as needed.
189. **Financial Intermediary**: An entity, like a bank, that works between savers and borrowers by accepting deposits and making loans.
190. **Fiscal Policy**: Operations by the Fed that affect the money supply including manipulation of the federal funds interest rate and the reserve requirement.

191. **Fractional Reserve Banking System**: A banking system wherein less than 100% of the deposits are required to be held as reserves.

192. **Government Bonds**: Bonds issued by the government and bought and sold by the Fed as a form of monetary policy to manipulate the money supply.

193. **Inflation:** An increase in the price level over time.

194. **Interest**: Money paid by a borrower to a lender in return for the use of money in the form of a loan.

195. **Interest Rate**: The rate of interest in the form of percent of the balance due per year.

196. **Lender**: One who gives money to be repaid at a later date, with interest?

197. **Liabilities**: Money owed.

198. **Loans**: Money given by lenders to borrowers.

199. **Monetary Policy:** Policy used to affect the money supply employed by the **Fed**. In particular, this describes the open market operations of buying and selling government bonds.

200. **Money**: The stock of assets used in transactions within an economy.

201. **Money Multiplier:** The number that describes the change in the money supply given an initial deposit and a reserve requirement.

202. **Money Supply:** The total amount of currency in circulation as controlled by Fed policy.

203. **Open Market Operations:** The purchase and sale of government bonds by the Fed in order to affect the money supply.

204. **Paper Balances:** Deposits that exist on paper but are not backed by physical currency.

205. **Principle:** The initial amount of money given as a loan.

206. **Reserve:** Money not given out in loans that is available for repaying depositors.

207. **Reserve Requirement:** The percent of total deposits required to be held back for repaying depositors. This is controlled by the Fed as a form of monetary policy.

208. **Savers:** Individuals who deposit money in banks.

209. **Treasury:** The government agency that prints, mints, and stores money.

ECONOMIC GROWTH

210. **Capital:** Physical and intellectual property that is utilized by labor in the production of goods and services.
211. **Capital Expenditure:** Money spent on increasing the amount of capital in a firm or an economy.
212. **Capital Stock:** The total amount of capital in an economy or in a firm.
213. **Convergence:** The theory that all industrialized countries tend to approach one another over time in terms of GDP per capita.
214. **GDP per Capita:** Nominal GDP divided by the total population. This indicates the amount of a country's total output that each member of the population theoretical has access to.
215. **Golden Rule Level of Capital:** The level of capital where consumption and savings are optimized.
216. **Growth Level:** The long term rate of growth.
217. **Growth Rate:** The short term rate of growth.
218. **Human Capital:** Intellectual property, like education and scientific discoveries that affects the level of output in a firm or country.
219. **Industrialized:** Describes countries that have an infrastructure and government amenable to industrial development.
220. **Infrastructure:** Physical machinery and transportation that is in place to aid in industrialization.
221. **International Market:** The market for goods and services that spans countries.
222. **Labor:** Workers who utilize capital to produce output.

223. **Labor Productivity Growth:** An increase in the amount of output a given unit of labor can produce.
224. **Nominal GDP:** The total currency value of all goods and services produced in a national economy.
225. **Open Market:** A market for the sale and purchase of goods and services in which all countries may compete.
226. **Output:** Goods and services produced by firms.
227. **Physical Capital:** Machinery used by labor in the production of goods and services.
228. **Production:** The creation of output.
229. **Production Capabilities:** The capital that allows a given amount of potential output.
230. **Productivity:** The ability to produce output.
231. **Prosperity:** The creation of a high standard of living.
232. **Savings Rate:** The percentage of total income that is saved for future consumption.
233. **Standard of living:** The level of economic wellbeing enjoyed by members of a population.
234. **Technological Progress:** The advancement of technology over time due to scientific discoveries.

AGREGATED DEMAND AND SUPPLY

235. **Aggregate Demand:** The total demand for goods and services in an economy.

236. **Aggregate Supply:** The total supply of goods and services in an economy.

237. **Crowding In:** When government spending induces private investment.

238. **Crowding Out:** When government spending reduces private investment.

239. **Demand Curve:** A schedule that relates price to quantity demanded.

240. **Disposable Income:** Income that may be spent after taxes are subtracted.

241. **Exogenous:** A change resulting from conditions outside of an economic model.

242. **GDP:** Gross domestic product is the total value of all goods and services produced within an economy.

243. **Income:** Money taken in by a system, an individual, a firm, or an economy.

244. **Inflation:** The year-to-year increase in the price level.

245. **Marginal Propensity to Consume:** A number that describes the amount of an additional dollar of income that a consumer will spend rather than save.

246. **Money Supply:** The total amount of currency and demand deposits that exists in an economy.

247. **National Income:** The total amount of money earned in an economy in a year. C.f. GDP.

248. **Net Exports:** The difference between exports and imports.

249. **Nominal Interest Rate:** The cost of borrowing money, unadjusted for inflation.

250. **Nominal Value:** The value of something in current currency, unadjusted for inflation.

251. **Output:** The amount of goods and services produced in an economy. This can be in quantity or in currency.

252. **Price Level:** The overall level of prices within an economy.

253. **Real Exchange Rate:** The rate that goods and services of one country can be traded for goods and services of another country.

254. **Real Interest Rate:** The cost of borrowing money, adjusted for inflation.

255. **Real Value:** The value of something in constant currency, adjusted for inflation.

TAX AND FISCAL POLICY

256. **Contractionary Fiscal Policy:** Policy enacted by the government that reduces output. Examples include raising taxes and decreasing government spending.

257. **Contractionary Monetary Policy:** Policy enacted by the Fed that reduces the money supply and thus reduces output. Examples include selling government bonds, raising the reserve requirement, and raising the federal funds interest rate.

258. **Currency:** Physical money used in an economy.

259. **Demand Deposits:** Money in a bank that can be withdrawn at any time, that is, on demand.

260. **Deposits:** Assets placed in a bank for storage and profit.

261. **Disposable Income:** Income that can be spent after taxes.

262. **Expansionary Fiscal Policy:** Policy enacted by the government that increases output. Examples include lowering taxes and increasing government spending.

263. **Expansionary Monetary Policy:** Policy enacted by the Fed that increases the money supply and thus increases output. Examples include purchasing government bonds, lowering the reserve requirement, and lowering the federal funds interest rate.

264. **The Fed:** Short for the Federal Reserve, the government agency that controls monetary policy.

265. **Federal Funds Interest Rate:** The rate that banks pay to borrow money from branches of the Fed.

266. **Fiscal Policy:** Policy that uses taxation and government spending to steer the economy.

267. **Fractional Reserve Banking System**: A system of banking, like in the US, where only a portion of deposits are help in reserves. The rest is returned to the public as loans, thereby

increasing the money supply and stimulating economic growth.

268. **Government Bonds:** Bonds issued by the government and sold by the Fed during open market operations as a means of monetary policy.

269. **Government Spending:** Money that the government spends on goods and services like employees, social security, and defense.

270. **Government Spending Multipliers:** Numbers that increase the change in output affected by a change in government spending due to consumer's marginal propensity to consume.

271. **Interest Rate:** The rate paid to lenders by borrowers in return for the use of a sum of money.

272. **Marginal Propensity to Consume:** A number that describes the amount of an additional dollar of income that a consumer will spend rather than save.

273. **Monetary Policy:** Policy enacted by the Fed to affect output. The three basic types include performing open market operations, changing the reserve requirement, and manipulating the federal funds interest rate.

274. **Money:** A means of exchange, store of value, and unit of account within an economy.

275. **Money Multiplier:** The number that describes the total change in the money supply resulting from a single deposit in a bank under a fractional reserve banking system.

276. **Money Supply:** The total amount of money in an economy including both demand deposits and currency.

277. **Multipliers:** Numbers that dictate the overall effect of a policy change on the output of an economy.

278. **National Income:** Output. (See the definition of output.)

279. **Open Market Operations:** The purchase and sale of government bonds by the Fed as a form of monetary policy.

280. **Output:** The total amount of goods and services produced within an economy in a given period of time.

281. **Price Level:** The overall level of prices within an economy.

282. **Real Output:** The total amount of goods and services produced within an economy in a given period of time valued in constant currency.

283. **Reserve Requirement:** The percentage of deposits that banks are required to keep in reserves and not give out as loans. This can be manipulated by the Fed under monetary policy.

284. **Tax Multipliers:** Numbers that describe the overall change in output created by a change in taxes due to fiscal policy change.

285. **Taxes:** Money collected by the government to maintain its services.

286. **Theory of Money Demand:** This basically states that as the demand for money increases, so does the interest rate.

287. **Stabilization policies:** Monetary policy aimed at reducing fluctuations in inflation and unemployment levels, while simultaneously maximizing national income. Such policies (out of favor in the era of globalization) attempt to expand demand when unemployment is high, and to curtail demand when inflation accelerates. Just remember the word stabilize. When a swing is rocking too much, you stabilize it. That's what happens when our economy is going up and down to fast.

288. **Countercyclical Policies:** Government policy aimed at reducing or neutralizing anti-social effects of economic cycles. Such policies encourage spending during downturns, and tighten credit during inflationary periods. Just remember counter! It is to stop bad things that affect our economy badly such as war in the Middle East that could jack up oil price, which in turn scares people from driving and going places because of perceived oil prices going up.

289. **Fiscal Policy:** Government's revenue (taxation) and spending policy designed to (1) counter economic cycles in order to

achieve lower unemployment, (2) achieve low or no inflation, and (3) achieve sustained but controllable economic growth. Just remember that this policy is important during recessions/inflations.

290. **John Maynard Keynes:** (1883-1946) argued that there was a "fundamental psychological law" concerning the relationship between income and consumption. John Maynard Keynes was, arguably, the most influential economist of the 20th century. He believed that government should act as a mediator between businesses and consumers as well as a watchdog.

291. **Keynesian Economics:** An economic theory of total spending in the economy and its effects on output and inflation.

292. **Nash Equilibrium:** A concept of game theory where the optimal outcome of a game is one where no player has an incentive to deviate from his or her chosen strategy after considering an opponent's choice. In other words, no player in the game would take a different action as long as every other player remains the same.

THE MOST COMMON GRAPHS

Production Possibilities Curve

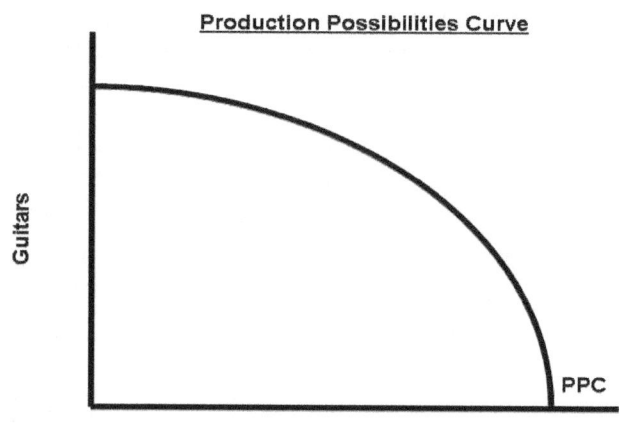

The PPC illustrates an economy's tradeoffs of producing different goods. This economy faces increasing opportunity costs (bowed outward).

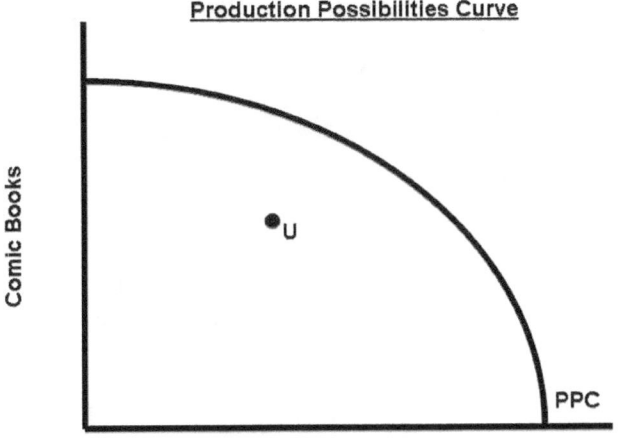

Point U represents unemployed resources and is inefficient.

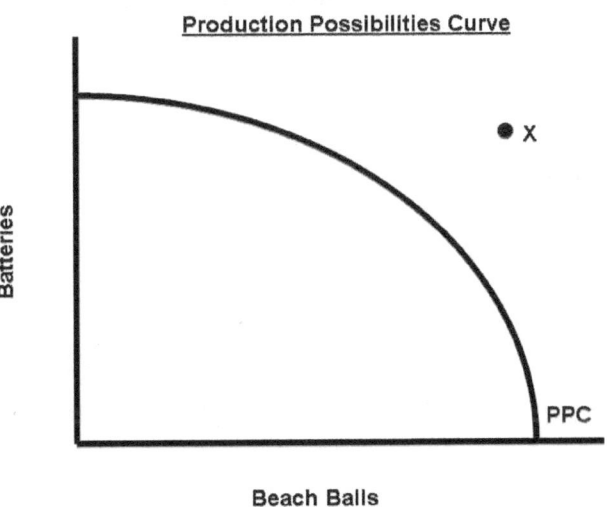

Point X is unattainable in the present.

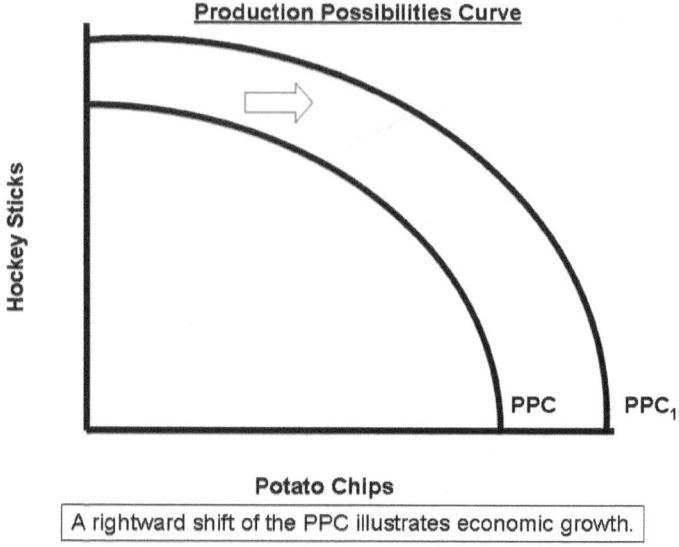

Summary: The Production Possibilities Curves above are concave to the origin which indicates the Law of Increasing Costs. The only way to produce beyond the curve is if economic growth occurs in the future or if the economy specializes and trades with another economy (Comparative Advantage). To simplify things, the PPC will be straight (constant cost) on the test to determine if trade should occur between two countries.

Supply And Demand Graphs

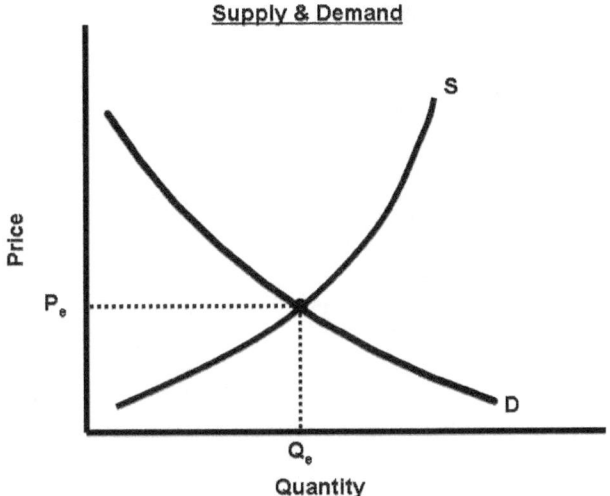

Equilibrium in any market exists where the demand curve intersects supply.

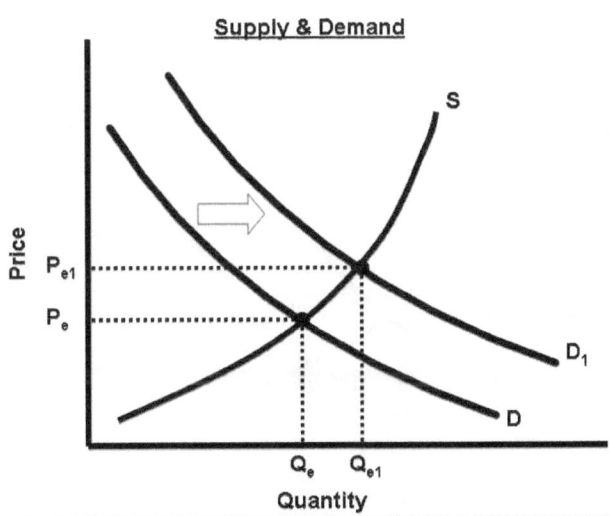

When demand shifts right, market price and quantity both increase.

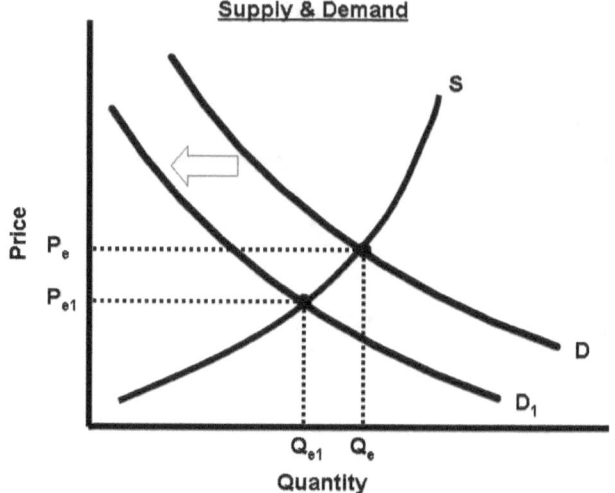

When demand shifts left, market price and quantity both decrease.

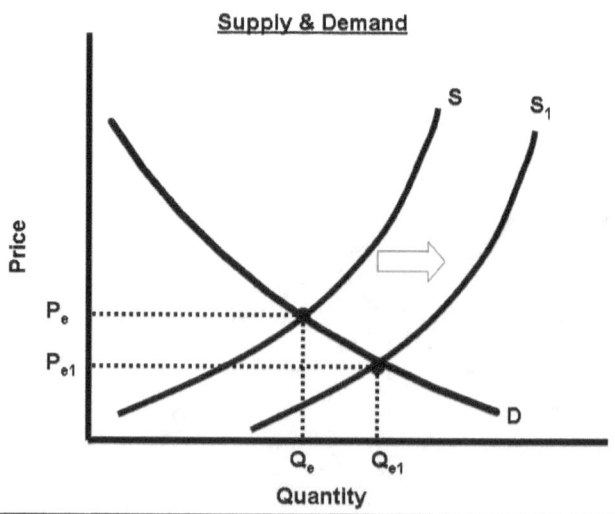

When supply shifts right, market price decreases and quantity increases.

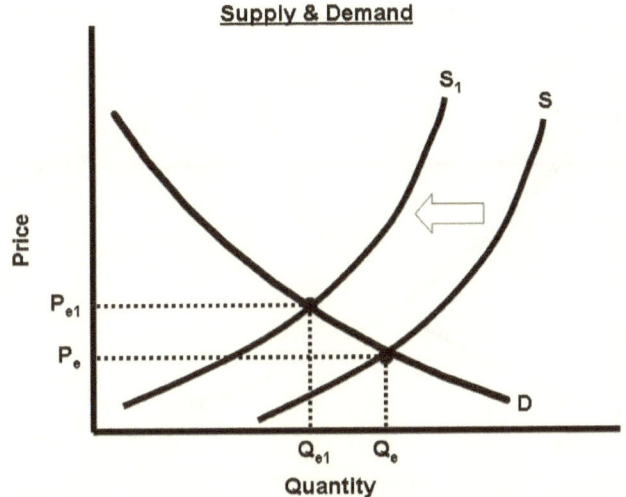

When supply shifts left, market price increases and quantity decreases.

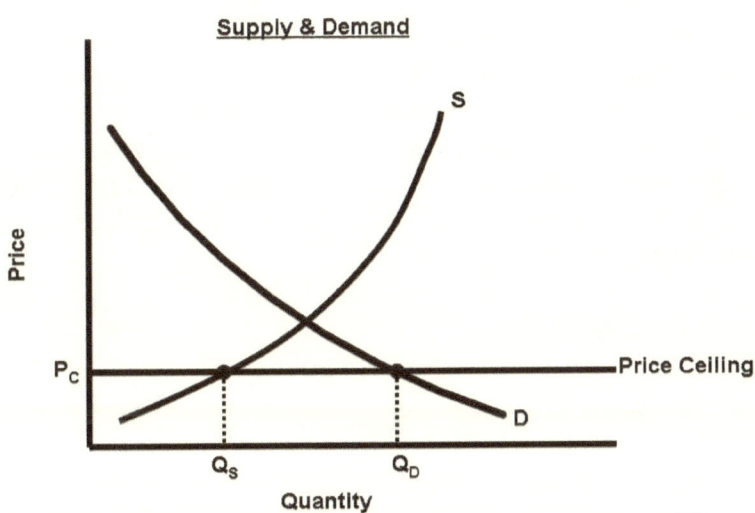

An effective Price Ceiling leads to a greater quantity demanded than quantity supplied causing a **shortage** of the good.

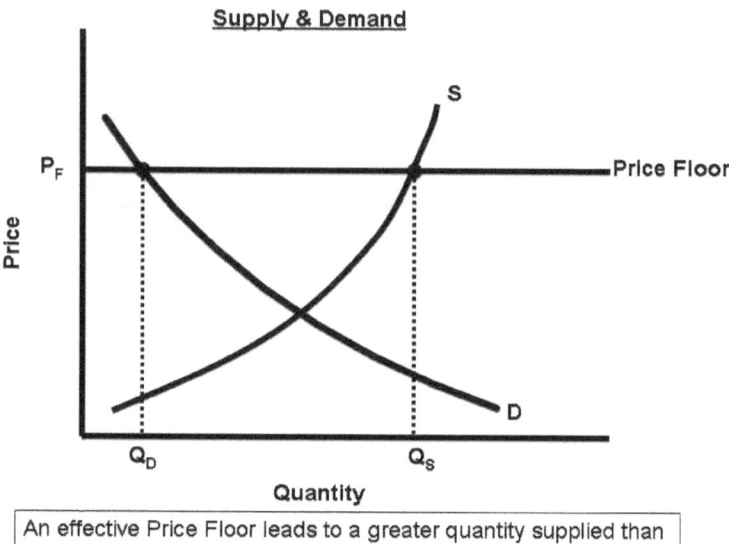

An effective Price Floor leads to a greater quantity supplied than quantity demanded causing a **surplus** of the good.

Summary: Remember, the non-price demand shifters are **T**astes and preferences, **I**ncome, **M**arket size, **E**xpectations of prices in the future, and **R**elated goods (the prices of substitutes and compliments). The key supply shifters are **R**esource prices, **E**xpectations of prices, **A**ctions of the government, and **P**roductivity. If dealing with simultaneous shifts of the demand and supply schedules, one variable will be indeterminate. When the government steps in to control prices a misallocation of resources results in the form of shortages and surpluses.

Circular Flow Model

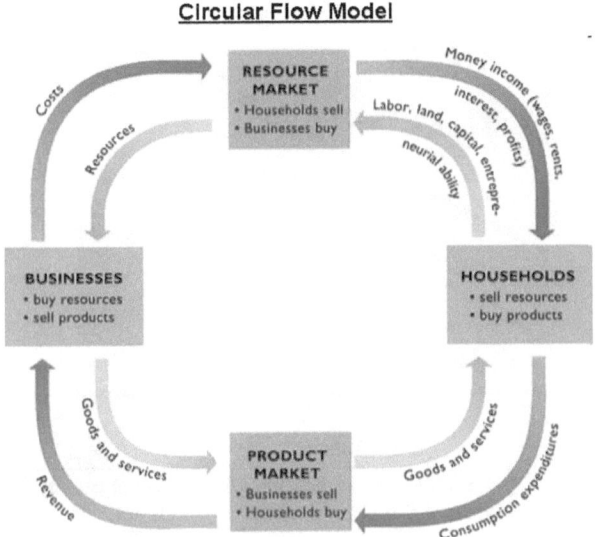

Summary: Above is the Circular Flow diagram from your textbook. Generally, you do not have to draw this on the AP exam, but you should know it inside and out for the multiple choice part.

Aggregate Expenditures Model

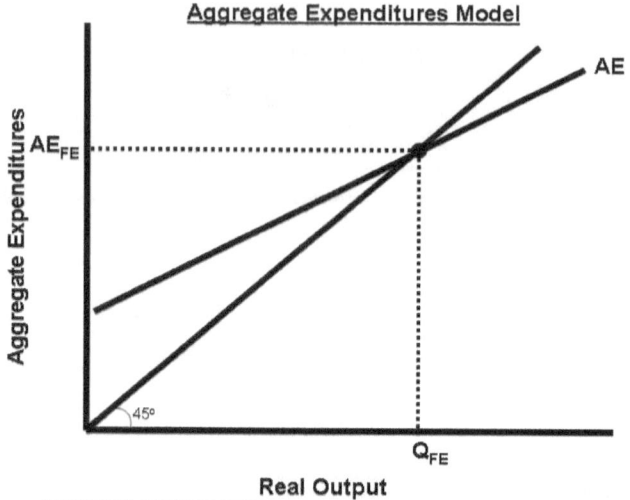

An economy operating at its full employment level of output. AE intersects the 45° line at full employment.

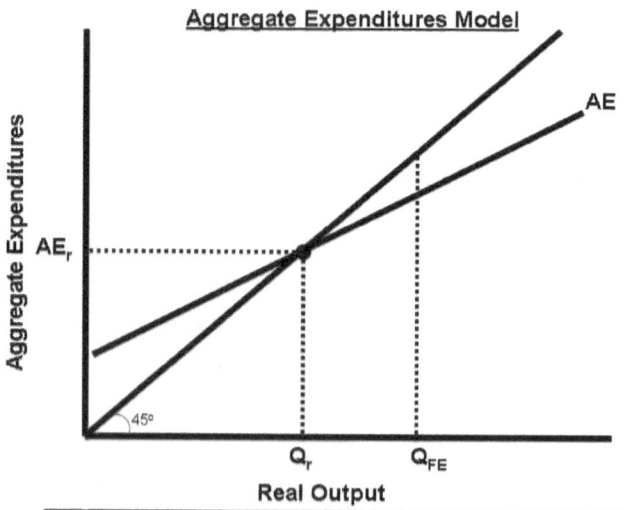

This economy is currently experiencing a recessionary gap. AE intersects the 45° line before full employment output.

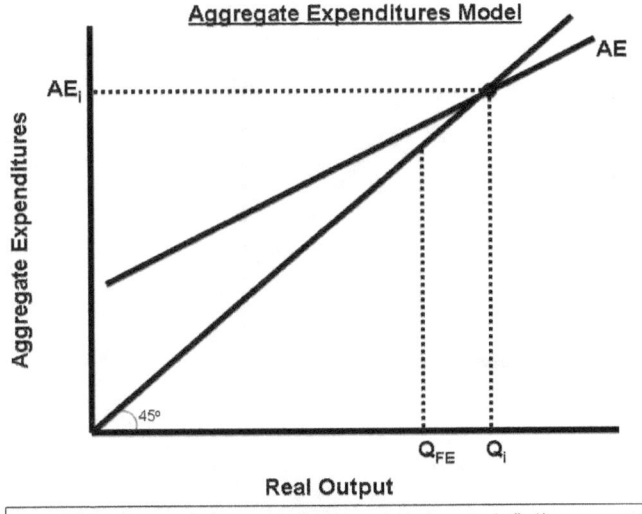

This economy is currently experiencing an inflationary gap. AE intersects the 45° line beyond the full employment level of output.

Summary: You will have to interpret Aggregate Expenditures on the multiple choice section. You can use this model to determine the state of the economy, the spending multiplier, and the amount of expenditures required to shift the AE curve to full employment.

Aggregate Demand and Aggregate Supply

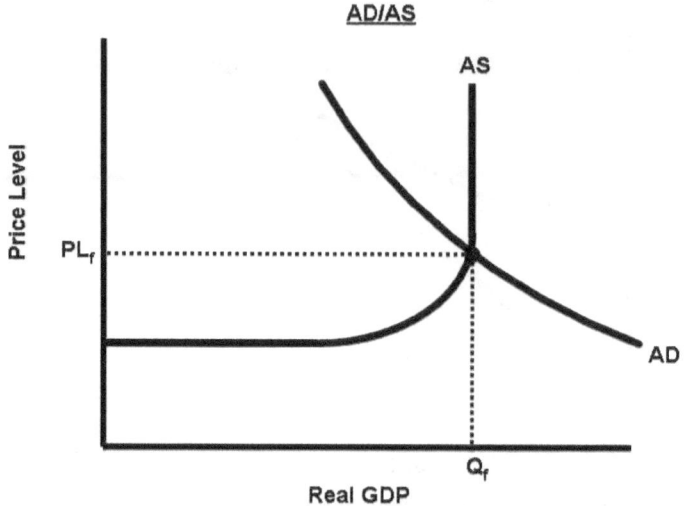

This economy is currently operating at its **full employment** level of output. AD crosses the very bottom of the classical range of the AS curve.

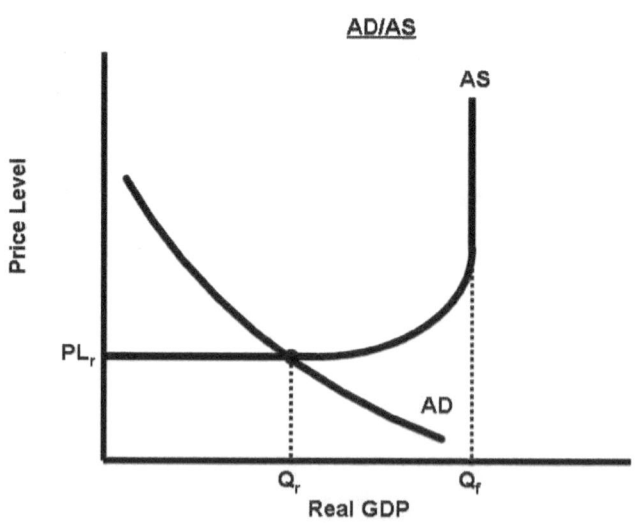

This economy is currently experiencing a **recession**. AD crosses the Keynesian range of the AS curve.

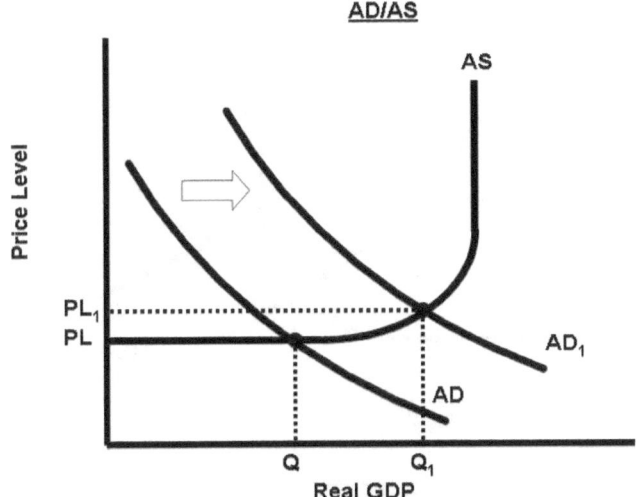

Expansionary fiscal or monetary policy will shift AD to the right, resulting in a higher price level, greater output, and lower unemployment.

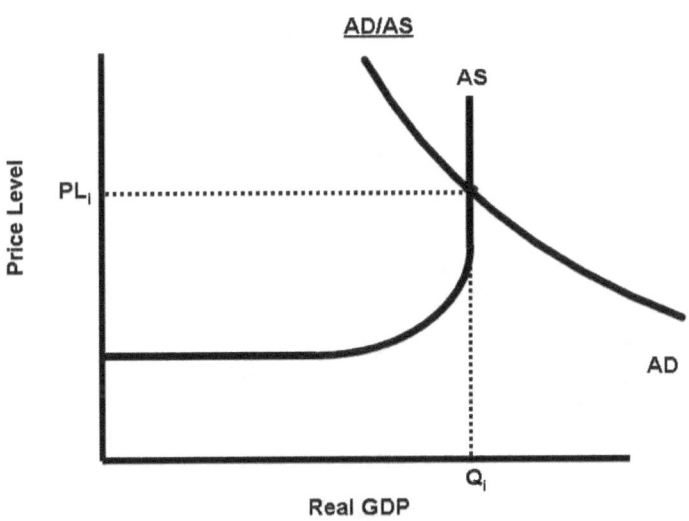

This economy is currently experiencing **inflation**. AD intersects a high level of the classical range of the AS curve.

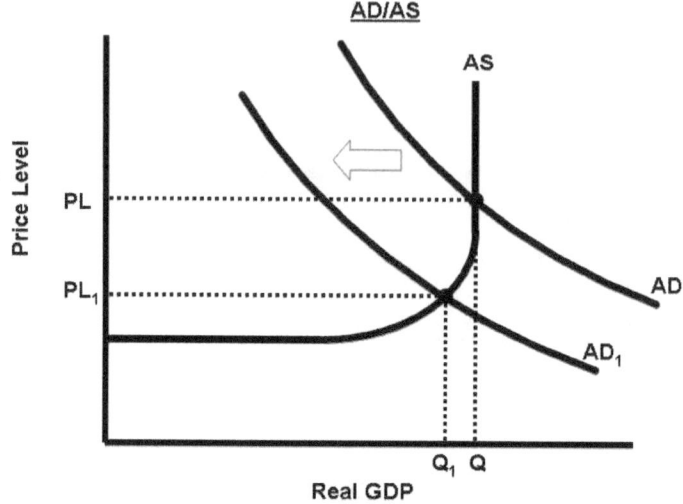

Contractionary fiscal or monetary policy will shift AD to the left, resulting in a lower price level, lower output, and increased unemployment.

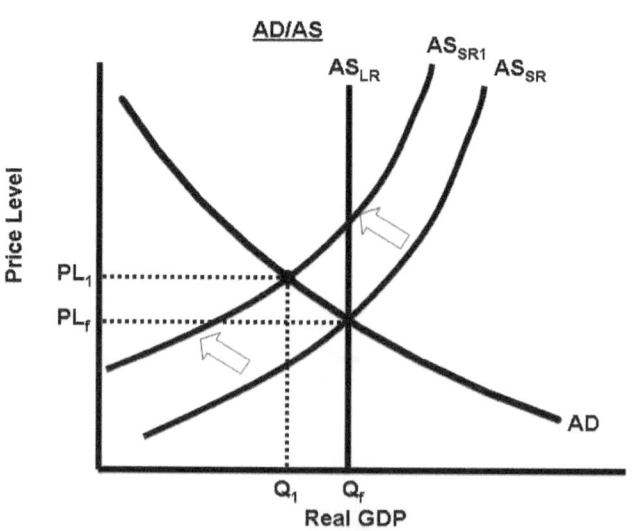

This economy is currently experiencing **stagflation**. AS_{SR} shifted left causing simultaneous inflation and recession.

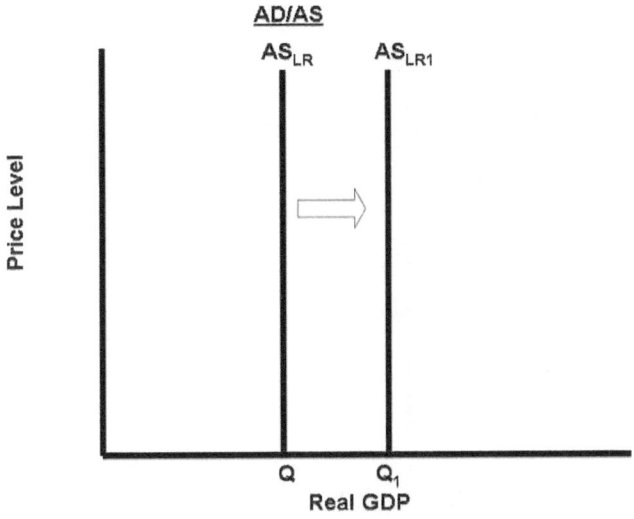

A rightward shift of long run aggregate supply illustrates economic growth.

Summary: When drawing the Aggregate Demand and Aggregate Supply graphs, don't forget to keep GDP Real on the horizontal axis. Use AD/AS when showing the current state of the economy, the results of Fiscal Policy, or the results of Monetary Policy. Shift aggregate demand for such policies or any change in Consumption, Investment, Government, or Xn. Shift short run aggregate supply when there is a change in Resource prices (such as oil), Actions of government (like subsidies to businesses), or Productivity.

Money Market Graphs

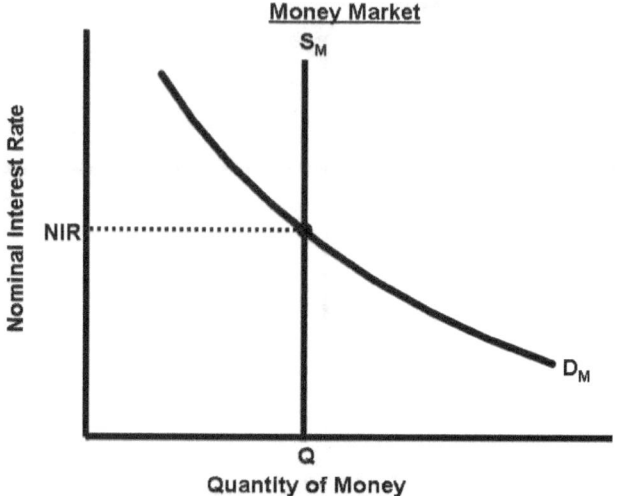

This money market is currently in equilibrium.
The money demand intersects the vertical money supply.

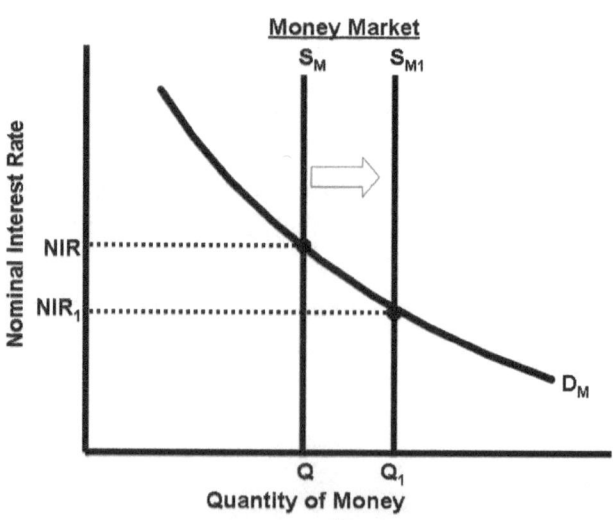

The Fed buys bonds causing an increase in the MS.
Nominal interest rates decrease as a result of **easy monetary policy**.

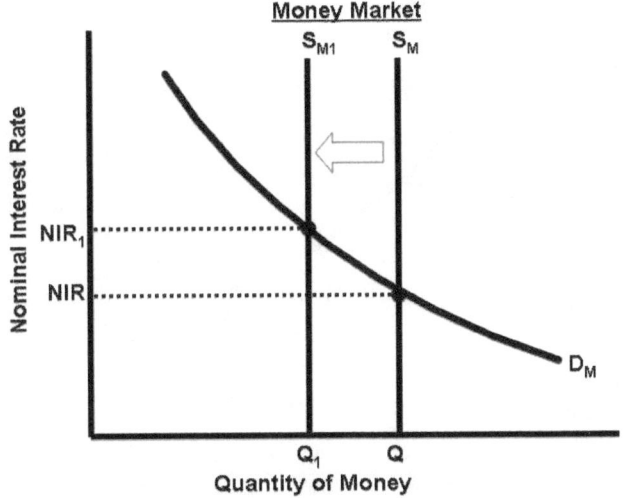

The Fed sells bonds causing a decrease in the MS. Nominal interest rates increase as a result of **tight monetary policy**.

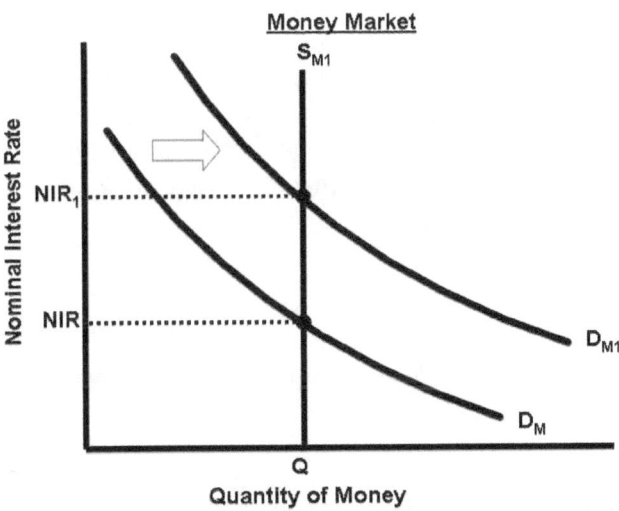

The demand for money increases as households decide to spend more money. Nominal interest rates increase as a result of these consumer expenditures.

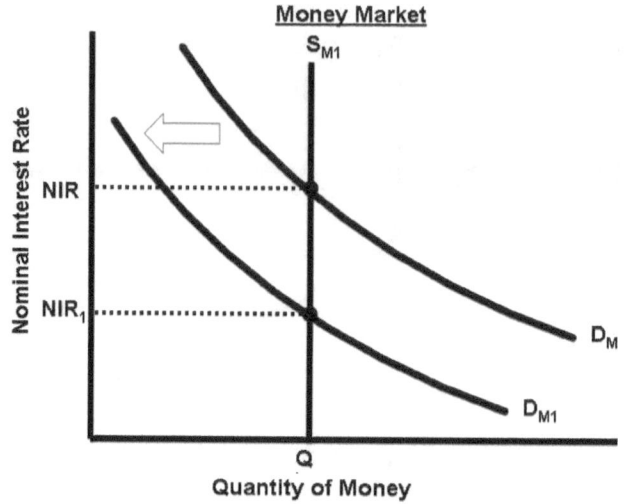

The demand for money decreases as households decide to spend less money. Nominal interest rates decrease due to lower consumer income (Recession).

Summary: The trick with drawing the Money Market is to remember that the supply of money is always vertical since it is set by Fed policymakers. If the Federal Reserve decides to buy/sell bonds, raise/lower reserve ratio, or raise/lower the discount rate then the supply of money will shift. If the Fed does nothing and consumer decisions change as a result of current economic conditions then you want to shift the demand for money instead. Also, make sure interest rates are nominal on the vertical axis.

Investment Demand Graphs

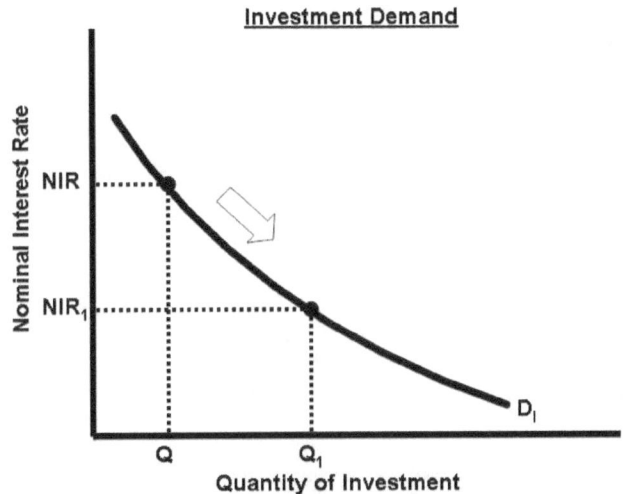

Quantity of investment increases when the nominal interest rate decreases.

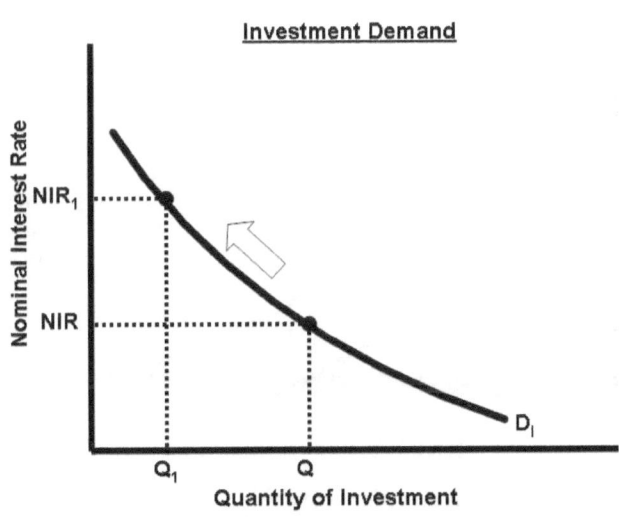

Quantity of investment decreases when the nominal interest rate increases.

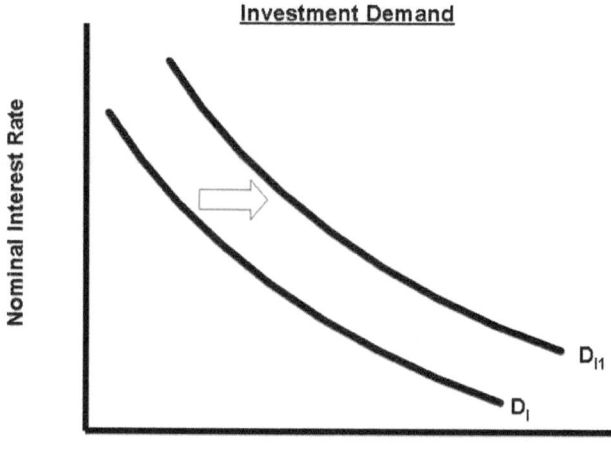

Investment demand shifts right (increases) when businesses are optimistic about future business conditions.

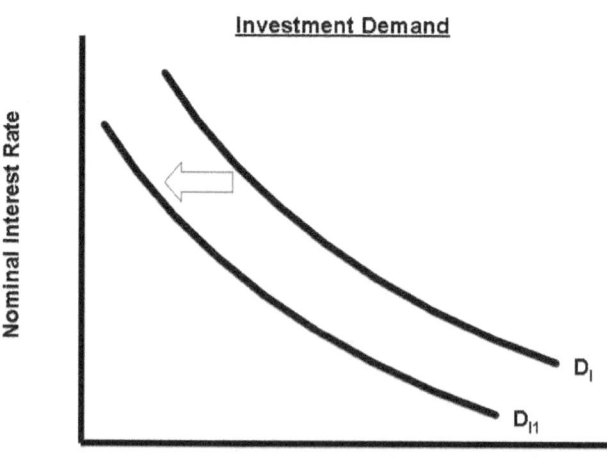

Investment demand shifts left (decreases) when businesses are pessimistic about future business conditions.

Summary: You can use the Investment Demand graph side-by-side with the Money Market to illustrate the relationship between Monetary Policy, nominal interest rates, and investment spending. Remember, changes in interest rates do not because a shift in the demand schedule, you simply slide to a different point on the curve. A major cause for the shift of the investment demand curve is the future business outlook.

Loanable Funds Market

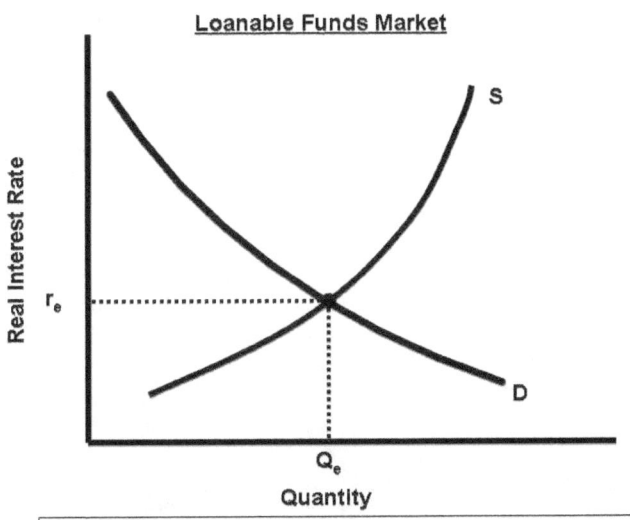

Equilibrium exists where the demand curve intersects supply.

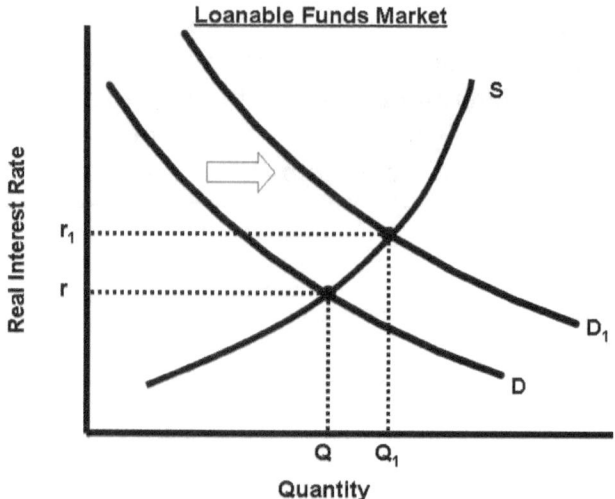

An increase government spending increases demand for loanable funds. Real interest rates increase which will crowd out private spending.

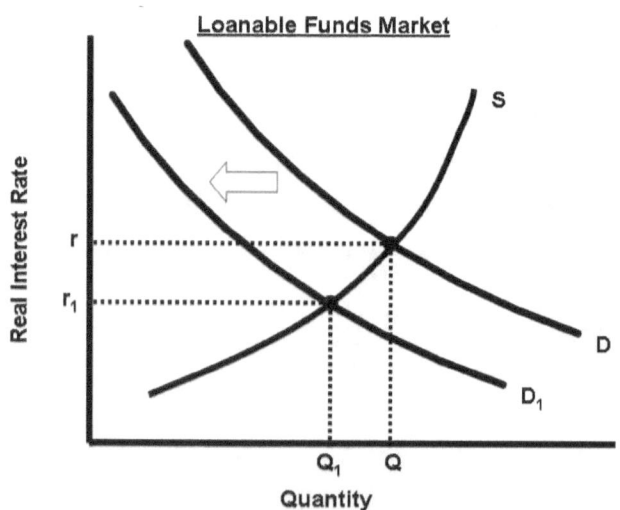

A decrease in government spending causes the demand to shift left. The real interest rate and quantity of loanable funds will both decrease.

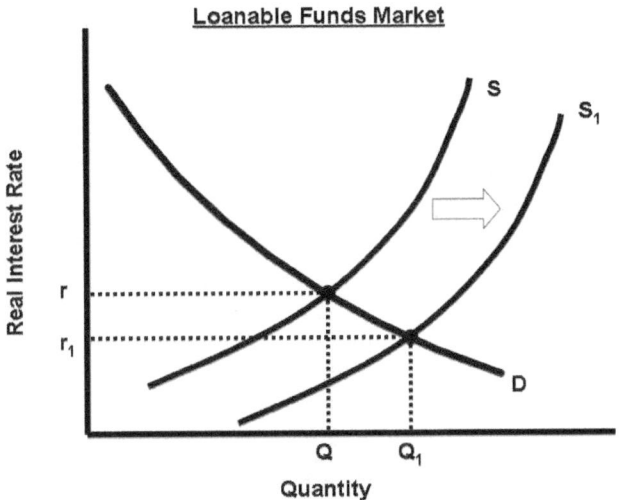

If households increase savings then the supply will increase.
Real interest rates will decrease and the quantity of loanable funds will increase.

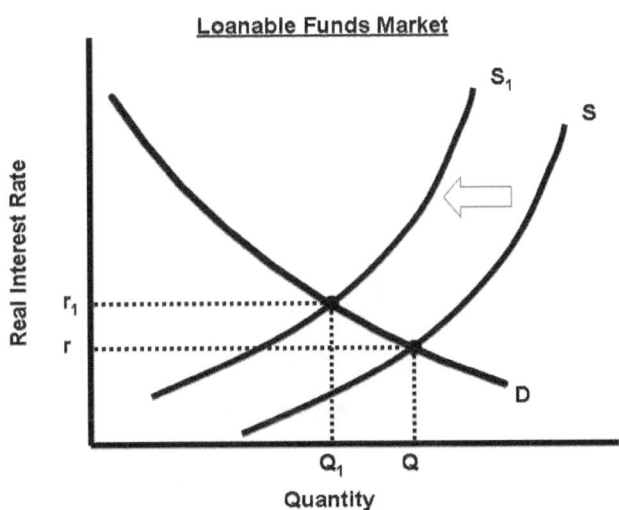

If households save less then the supply of loanable funds shifts left.
Real interest rates will increase and the quantity will decrease.

Summary: Use the Loanable Funds Market when illustrating a change in government spending (deficit spending which leads to the infamous "crowding out effect") or when households change their savings habits. Remember to keep that interest rate real on the vertical axis.

www.ingramcontent.com/pod-product-compliance
Lightning Source LLC
Chambersburg PA
CBHW020711180526
45163CB00008B/3033